Red Eyed Tree Frogs as Pets

A Complete Red Eyed Tree Frog Care Guide

Red Eyed Tree Frog breeding, where to buy, types, care, temperament, cost, health, handling, diet, and much more included!

By: Lolly Brown

Foreword

Fast gaining in popularity among frog and amphibian enthusiasts is the Red-eyed Tree Frog. With their beautiful and distinctive coloring, their calm and placid natures, and their low maintenance care, these unique rainforest frogs have found their way into homes all over the country and worldwide.

This is not a pet for novice frog keepers. While they are generally considered low-maintenance pets compared to other exotic amphibians and pets, they do require specialized care. Don't bring one home unless you've done your research and decided that you are quite capable of providing one of these little creatures the kind of home and environment in which it can thrive. Arm yourself with good information and care for these frogs well, and they can make satisfying frog pets and beautiful terrarium animals.

Table of Contents

Introduction

You've probably seen them before – center stage in posters and other media advocating rainforest preservation and conservation, and these colorful little green frogs do seem to have the charisma to pull it off. Who better to symbolize this movement, after all, than a beautiful and popular frog belonging to an ecological indicator species and whose primary habitat is, in fact, the steadily dwindling tropical rainforests?

Frogs in general have been historically are considered as ecological indicators, and the state of their presence a reflection of the state of the ecosystem itself. While we may all recognize the steadily dwindling areas of rainforests in the world at a remove level of consciousness, deforestation is given a whole new meaning when one also learns that frogs and amphibian species the world over have been steadily diminishing in numbers, with some species becoming extinct altogether in recent years. Numerous animals are becoming endangered due to the encroaching loss of habitat, and this warning has been put on high alert among conservation groups the world over because of the diminishing frog and amphibian populations all over the world.

The Red-eyed Tree Frog itself is not considered threatened – its official conservation status at present is that of "least concern"- but this is mainly due to the efforts of captive breeders who have succeeded wonderfully in breeding a fair number of Red-eyed Tree Frogs in captivity. This does not reflect their state in their natural habitat, however, since many Red-eyed Tree Frogs in the wild are vulnerable due to loss of habitat, predatory threats, chemical contamination, increased UV exposure due to a weakened ozone layer, and the recent proliferation of a fatal infection among various frog species.

Thus the steady advocacy for rainforest preservation and conservation, for which this amazing and unique frog species has been the recognizable symbol.

In a way, it could be argued that keeping and caring for one of these frogs in your own home is one of the best ways of promoting awareness of rainforest preservation efforts.

Glossary of Red-eyed Tree Frog Terms

Advertisement Call – mating call of frogs

Aggressive Call – territorial warning among male frogs; also "territorial call"

Amphibian – Vertebrates that spend part of their lives in water as well as on land. Other amphibians include salamanders and caecilians.

Amplexus – When a male positions himself on top of a female in order to fertilize her eggs

Anura – "tail-less"

Army – a group of frogs

Carnivore – meat-eater, including insectivores

Chorus – a large congregation of calling frogs

Chytridiomycosis – Also sometimes known as BD, a fungus that is deadly to most frogs

Cloaca – Opening in the rear end of a frog which allows for the passage of waste products, eggs, and sperm

Detritus – decayed plant and animal matter that collects at the bottom of a pond or water

Distress Call – call made to discourage predators

Ectothermic – external or environmental means of regulating body temperature

Frog – Any tailless amphibian of the order Anura

Froglet – a young frog that has just finished its metamorphosis from a tadpole

Herpetology – study of reptiles and amphibians

Insectivore – insect eater

Larva – Immature form or life-stage of amphibians

Metamorphosis – Profound change from one life stage to another, e.g., when tadpoles undergo a change and become frogs

Nictitating Membrane – a transparent inner eyelid

Pollywog – tadpoles

Frogspawn – collective term for frog eggs

Tadpole – larval stage of a frog's life cycle

Toe Pads – fleshy, disc-shaped sticky toes of tree frogs

Tympanum – The frog's eardrum

Vernal Pools – Temporary ponds formed with seasonal water such as snow melt or spring rains

Vocal Sac – skin pouches under a frog's chin that are inflated in order to make a call

Chapter One: Understanding Red-eyed Tree Frogs

More commonly known as the Red-eyed Tree Frog, this frog species bears the scientific sounding name of Agalychnis callidryas, which is actually derived from Greek *kallos* (beautiful) and *dryas* (tree or wood nymph). And it is not so difficult to imagine why this beautiful and vividly colored tree-dwelling frog species has been named for Greek mythology's dryads or wood nymphs – forest spirits that appear and disappear at will, and are known for their dainty physique and beautiful appearance. There does seem to be a kind of magic in this frog species' personality, for they have since gained popularity among frog keepers and enthusiasts, and have even landed the lead role for poster-frog for the advocacy of rainforest preservation and conservation.

They are also sometimes called "monkey frogs," and this moniker serves to highlight another aspect of their character – they are wonderful and agile jumpers as they navigate their way through the dense forest canopies where they make their primary habitat. Nimble and agile, startling and beautiful, they do seem to fit their original comparison to dryads quite well.

While not a frog species recommended for beginners, the fascination with and popularity of Red-eyed Tree Frogs is very real. This steady rise in popularity as a household pet has had one fortunate turn – captive breeding efforts have ensured that this amphibian species, at least, is in the clear while the populations of many amphibian and frog species all over the world are becoming endangered.

Facts About Red-eyed Tree Frogs

These tea-cup sized frogs hail from tropical rainforest areas located variously in southern Mexico, central America, and northern South America. They are well-known for their vivid coloring, including the startling big red eyes for which they have been named – a trait they use quite effectively as a measure of protection and self-defense in what is known as "startle coloration." By a sudden display of their bright and vivid colors, especially their eyes, they can make use of the momentary distraction caused the would-be predator to get away.

Red-eyed Tree Frogs are nocturnal and arboreal, which means that they are active mostly at night, and that they live mostly in the canopy or foliate of trees. As with all amphibians, however, they do spend part of their lifetime in water when they are still newly-hatched tadpoles. What follows in their life cycle is the fascinating metamorphosis of the larvae with gills and a tail into a land and tree-dwelling frog with legs the legs and lungs of a frog. While younger froglets are brown in color, with adulthood and maturity come the unique coloration for which this species are known.

This is a mostly calm and quiet species except during breeding season when they can get a bit croaky. They are also non-poisonous, which is another reason they make such ideal pets. The prospective keeper is advised, however, that this frog does not tolerate too much handling and is better observed through the clear glass of their artificial homes.

Summary of Red-eyed Tree Frog Facts

Basic Red-eyed Tree Frog Information

Scientific Name: Agalychnis callidryas

Kingdom: Animalia

Phylum: Chordata

Class: Amphibia

Order: Anura

Family: Hylidae

Genus: Agalychnis

Species: A. callidryas

Regions of Origin: Southern Mexico, Central America, northern South America, including southern Veracruz, Oaxaca in Mexico, central and eastern Panama, northern Colombia, southwestern Nicaragua, and southwestern Costa Rica

Primary Habitat: Near rivers and ponds in rainforests, humid and tropical lowlands

Description: The body is primarily a vibrant green color, with yellow and blue vertical stripes; it has webbed feet and toes which are orange/red. As per its name, it has red eyes with vertical narrow pupils.

Primary Behavioral Characteristics: Nocturnal, communal frogs, arboreal, and carnivorous

Health Conditions: Oodinium, Red Leg Disease, Metabolic Bone Disease, Chytrid Fungus

Lifespan: average of 5 years, but may live longer

Origin and Distribution

First identified in the 1860s by herpetologist Edward Cope, The Red Eyed Tree Frog, or the Agalychnis callidryas, is native to the humid rainforests in countries such as Belize, Colombia, Costa Rica, Guatemala, Honduras, Mexico, Nicaragua, Panama, as well as northern parts of Southern America. This is an arboreal hylid, or a tree-dwelling amphibian, and its natural habitat can be located near water sources such as rivers, ponds and streams in rainforest areas and in humid or tropical lowlands.

They are not considered endangered and its status as classified by the International Union for Conservation of Nature (IUCN) Red List is that of Least Concern, though their natural habitat is being threatened by logging, deforestation, and other environmental issues. More recently, or in 2010, the Agalychnis callidryas was placed under CITES protection, under Appendix II.

Chapter Two: Things to Know Before Getting a Red-Eyed Tree Frog

The average lifespan of a Red-eyed Tree Frog is 5 -10 years, so if you are thinking of bringing one home, make sure that you are ready to make the commitment to care for your pet for the duration of its lifetime.

The good news is that these unique creatures are relatively low maintenance pets, though like with most other frogs and amphibians, they will require regular care. You might not mind the brief daily interaction, feeding, and cage cleaning and maintenance that is involved, however, because you might never get tired of watching these visually stunning creatures. And of course, the privilege of being able to watch the growth, development and transformation of a frog throughout its lifetime right within your own home is a small but not insignificant spectacle in itself.

There are certain considerations that you will have to factor in before bringing a Red-eyed Tree Frog home, and knowing where to buy one or how to take care of it isn't the only thing to consider. In this chapter, we take a look at the some of the basic aspects of what it means to keep a Red-eyed Tree Frog as a pet as a kind of overview of what the next 5-10 years will be like for you if you do decide that this is the pet for you.

Do You Need a License?

Certain countries require a special license for frogs or amphibians, and a violation of such special laws can mean heavy fines. In the United States, licenses and permits for keeping pets, exotic or wild animals, and amphibians, are decided on the state level. So whether or not you need a license to keep a Red-eyed Tree Frog depends on the area where you live, and the prevailing laws in your state, municipality, and town.

Be sure to check not just your state laws, but also your town and even neighborhood laws just in case. It can happen that even when state law does not expressly prohibit the keeping of frogs as pets, your local neighborhood laws, or the laws in your local town or municipality may prohibit, restrict, or prescribe certain requirements before you can do so. So before you even do all the legwork of researching the species and looking for where these frogs may be sold, check whether or not there are any legal impediments to your keeping one. If a license or permit is required for keeping, transporting, purchasing, selling, and breeding amphibians such as the Red-eyed Tree Frogs, then of course you should do your best to comply. Pay attention to any restrictions, limitations or requirements prescribed by your local laws. This includes an almost universal prohibition against releasing captive pets into the wild.

In general, though, be aware that many territories at present prohibit the capture of wild frogs, or the trade or purchase of wild-caught frogs, to keep as pets – as opposed to the purchase, sale, and keeping of captive bred frogs. This is in keeping with minimizing the risks of the spread of the Chytrid Fungus that has already ravaged many amphibian species populations in the world.

How Many Red-eyed Tree Frogs Should You Keep?

The choice of how many Red-eyed Tree Frogs to keep
is a personal one, and you can certainly keep one or more if
you want to and understand the commitment and
responsibility that either choice entails. In general, however,
this is a communal frog, and you can easily house 3-4 of
these calm and placid species in a standard 20-gallon
terrarium.

While they may never be completely sociable with
you as their owner and dislike being handled too much or
too often, the Red-eyed Tree Frog is sociable enough with its
own species. Some would recommend one male to 2-3
females as a good ratio of a communal setup.

Do Red-eyed Tree Frogs Get Along with Other Pets?

The simplest and most practical answer to this
question is to simply keep your Red-eyed Tree Frog isolated
from all your other household pets. This minimizes any
"mistakes" or poor husbandry practices that might
ultimately adversely affect your frog.

For one thing, when it comes to the more general run-of-the-mill household pets such as cats and dogs, the interaction may not prove to be a wholesome one. Frogs are potential carriers of the Salmonella which, while it might not adversely affect them, can prove detrimental or even fatal to humans and other mammals. And secondly, the natural exuberance and curiosity of some mammalian pets such as cats or dogs that are used to social interaction will only unduly stress your little frog – a creature that is not overly fond of being handled at all. Too much stress on your frog is obviously not good, and it may eventually lead to the development of potential health conditions.

As to mixing different frog species, again, the smart thing to do would be to isolate each species, but in certain cases, mixing is possible. It is assumed here that you have done your research and none of the frog species you are proposing to mix are known to be aggressive or territorial, and that you are not proposing to mix wild caught frogs with captive-breds. It is further assumed that all of your frogs are in good health and have been duly checked by a professional veterinarian for possible diseases or bacteria they may be carrying. Please remember that the current epidemic of Chytrid Fungus infecting frog populations all over the world is one of the strongest arguments against mixing different frog populations together.

Presuming that none of the considerations above apply in your case, the main considerations you are facing now in mixing different frog species is a question of the size and suitability of habitat. Cramming frogs into a too-small enclosure does not make for healthy living conditions, since each species will need their own space. In addition, frogs hailing from different regions will necessarily require different types of habitat – from substrate, temperature, humidity, water levels, and equipment requirements. If these are not compatible, then do not mix your frogs.

Red-eyed Tree Frogs are also quite a gentle and fragile species, and there is no telling what might happen if you mix them with a different amphibian species in a confined area. Try not to mix different frog species with widely diverse size ranges – a 2-3 inch Red-eyed Tree Frog, for example, with a far larger species. Even if both species are gentle and placid by nature, there is simply no telling what might happen if you mix two different creatures in a confined environment. And if the other frog is far larger and more muscular, you won't have to guess which frog has the upper hand. Predation among amphibians is not unheard of. And even if your Red-eyed Tree Frog might not express its dissatisfaction eloquently – mixing species can be quite stressful for the involuntary inhabitants.

One other concern that most keepers express in arguing against mixing frog species together is the possibility of unexpected cross-breeding or hybrid frog mixes. Hybridization is frowned upon within the frog-keeping community because it lowers the predictability of the type of care that the hybrid frog requires.

It is possible to mix different frog species together in the same habitat, but this is generally only done by keepers and hobbyists with years of experience, thorough knowledge of the frogs they are keeping, and enough money for the needed large enclosure. If you are not sure about the suitability of the various factors that come into play when mixing two different species together, then it is best to err on the side of caution and simply keep different species in different tanks.

How Much Does it Cost to Keep a Red-eyed Tree Frog?

The cost of keeping and maintaining a pet frog is not very prohibitive – in fact, frogs are widely touted among pet owners for being low cost maintenance pets. Perhaps the one biggest investment you will have to make for your Red-eyed Tree Frog is their habitat, which can cost anywhere from $20-250, depending on what you are looking for and how impressive you want your set up to be.

Being an exotic species, the Red-eyed Tree Frog is a bit higher up on the scale of prices for pet frogs, on the average costing about $70-100. Aside from the food that you can purchase in bulk at your local pet store, and some funds set aside for emergency veterinary services, as long as you provide the proper environment or habitat, you and your frog are pretty much set.

During your first year, therefore, your cost expectations are quite moderate, and might look a little something like this:

Startup costs for a Pet Red-eyed Tree Frog	
Purchase price	$70-100
Tank or aquarium setup	$20-250
Total	$90-350

The subsequent long-term costs after your initial year are relatively low, mainly centering on the purchase of food which generally consists of live crickets. These are easily available at any pet store – a three-month supply can cost around $20 on the average. The average yearly cost of food for your frog, therefore, is around $80, though it can easily be cheaper if you manage to find a good deal.

What are the Pros and Cons of Keeping Red-eyed Tree Frogs as Pets

To sort of sum things up for you as you give final consideration to the overall advisability or inadvisability of keeping Red-eyed Tree Frogs as pets, below are a summary of the pros and cons of keeping these beautiful creatures as pets.

Each pet inevitably comes with their own pros and cons – and this is true for the more mainstream pets as it is for the more exotic ones. Consider the following points in terms of your own lifestyle and the demands of your life, what your expectations are in a pet frog, and why it is that you want to keep a Red-eyed Tree Frog in the first place. Consider also whether or not you will be in the position to care for these frogs long-term. If the care that these frogs require is not compatible with the life you lead, or if you were expecting a pet that you can interact more with, then perhaps the Red-eyed Tree Frog is not the right fit for you.

Pros for the Red-Eyed Tree Frog

- It can be an educational and enlightening experience to own a frog – not only for kids but also for adults. Watching a frog feed by catching a fly with its tongue, leap from branch to branch, or (especially if you have the opportunity of starting out with a tadpole) witness its metamorphosis and transformation from egg or tadpole to an adult frog.
- Requires little interaction and socialization, if this is what you are looking for. On the other hand, their vivid coloring and interesting behavior makes them wonderful pets to watch and observe.
- Placid and gentle creatures – not aggressive, temperamental, poisonous or dangerous.
- As long as you get the basic requirements of a suitable habitat, regular habitat maintenance, and feeding, right, this frog can pretty much be left on its own. In this sense, they are low maintenance and low cost pets.

Cons for the Red-eyed Tree Frog

- The initial start-up, including the terrarium or aquarium and the various equipment you will need to set it up just right (temperature, humidity, and environment) can be quite expensive
- While being low maintenance in terms of habitat cleaning, their terrarium does need some maintenance, and this can sometimes be a messy or even a smelly job. Keeping a frog in unclean surroundings will eventually adversely affect their health.
- This is not a pet that can and should be handled too often. So if what you are looking for is an interactive pet, this may not be the right pet for you.
- Can be a bit boring to watch – they are mostly nocturnal creatures, so they will probably do nothing while you are watching them during the day.
- Are quite fragile and delicate – should not be handled often, and even then, should never be touched with hands that might carry dangerous chemicals or other substances that can prove deadly to the frogs.
- Are insectivores, and needs live prey. You will need to handle live insects like crickets when feeding them, and you will probably need to keep a stock of live

crickets and other insects in the house. If this is not to your liking, then perhaps another pet or species will be better for you.

- Their care can be quite specific and needs some experience and knowledge. This is not an ideal pet for beginner frog keepers, but a great one for those at the "intermediate" level.

- It is not very easy to find a vet with experience in dealing with amphibians, let alone an exotic species of frog! You will either have to go a long way to find one, or spend quite a bit for their services.

Chapter Three: Purchasing Your Red-eyed Tree Frog

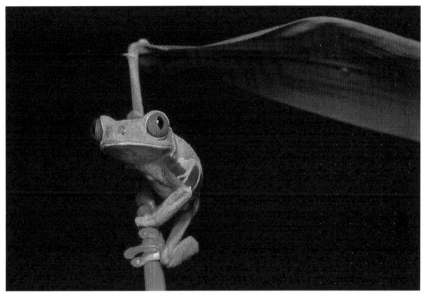

The good news is that this somewhat exotic Red-eyed Tree Frog is now widely available for any keeper or enthusiast wanting to bring one of these beautiful creatures home. Successful breeding programs over the past few years that have been geared towards reducing the incidence of the Chytrid Fungus, as well as reducing the incidence of wild-caught frogs, have thus eagerly bred this species in captivity, ensuring not only the frog's continued existence regardless of their conditions in the wild, but that there are more than a few to go around so that hobbyists need not look farther than the nearest breeder.

Just some of the places where you can find one of these frogs for sale are your local pet shops, online sellers, and reptile and amphibian shows. If you are the type who wants to see what you purchase before actually handing over money, then by all means attend an amphibian show, or you can visit the nearest pet shop that carries one of these frogs. You might want to devote more of your energy to attending an amphibian show, however. Not only does this bring you in contact with other hobbyists and enthusiasts that can answer your questions and educate you regarding the best way of caring for a frog, you will also most likely come into contact with the same breeder responsible for the life of the frog you have chosen. This is a magnificent networking and educational opportunity – and certainly a far cry from dealing with the more remote and likely uninvolved pet store staff. On the other hand, if you find a pet store that carries Red-eyed Tree Frogs, chances are that they will also carry many of the equipment, food and materials you will be needing for your frog.

Another option you may have is to look for online sellers or breeders that offer Red-eyed Tree Frogs for sale. It is always advisable to see the frog and to meet the breeder in person before actually making your purchase, but if this is not possible, then do your research before committing to the purchase of any one frog. Read online reviews, post questions in online forums to ask people about their recommendations regarding online breeders and sellers. Once you have narrowed down your list of reputable online sellers, make contact and don't hesitate to ask them questions. This is a good way for you to screen which are reputable breeders and to begin to form a polite acquaintanceship with another enthusiast whom you will likely wish to ask questions of later on.

How to Choose a Reputable Red-eyed Tree Frog Breeder

You will have to do your own research before you even begin looking for a reputable Red-eyed Tree Frog breeder. Knowing as much as you possibly can about this species allows you not only to converse intelligently with the breeder, but also allows you to ask intelligent questions of your own. This lowers the potential risk for dissatisfaction on either side. Remember that the breeder is screening you as a potential frog keeper as much as you are screening him or her as a reputable breeder.

Keep in mind that buying wild-caught frogs, or Red-eyed Tree Frogs caught directly from the wild, is not advisable for both health and environmental reasons. Assure yourself as much as you can, therefore, that the frogs being sold are not wild caught, and have not, in any case, been exposed to other frogs, whether of the same or different species, that were caught from the wild and have not undergone the required quarantine period. Again, dependable reviews from other and objective previous customers of the same breeder would go a long way in verifying the breeder's reputability, as you might not get a chance to see the frogs at all prior to the time when they are ready to be sold.

In any case, a reputable breeder would not only be willing but will actually be enthusiastic to discuss various information about the frogs with you, and will also be willing to share any advice on husbandry and possibly recount his own experiences. Pay attention, listen, do your own research, and trust your better judgment.

Tips for Selecting a Healthy Red-eyed Tree Frog

You will probably not be able to pick up the frogs to examine them prior to picking one out for yourself, and doing so is not really recommended. The Red-eyed Tree Frog was not really built for too much handling, and manually picking them up in order to inspect them can only ensure that you are bringing home a stressed-out frog, and probably leaving a couple of other stressed-out frogs with the breeder – and none of them will appreciate you for it.

It remains, therefore, for you to make your choice based only on your observations – how it looks, and how it behaves.

This may not always be so easy since Red-eyed Tree frogs are basically nocturnal, and unless you are picking one out after the sun goes down, you will probably be observing a frog that is simply sitting still and doing nothing during the entire course of its "audition." Health-wise, however, there are a few warning signs that you may wish to steer clear of:

- Beware of getting too thin frogs where the hip and backbones are already prominent. At the same time, steer clear of frogs whose abdomens look bloated. Either are a sign of poor nutrition, poor digestion, internal infections, bacterial edema, or even vitamin toxicity.
- Behavioral warning signs can include lethargy, not eating or jumping, and excessive weight loss. It's a good idea to ask the breeder to feed the frogs while you observe so that you can see which frogs are eating well and which seem to have no appetite.
- Familiarize yourself with pictures, images or even actual observations of the coloring and skin texture of Red-eyed Tree Frogs. Then when you try to pick out your frog, watch out for any discolorations, skin patches, and unusual reddish coloring on the frog's

thighs and belly. The latter could be a sign of Red Leg Disease.

- Cloudy or smoky eyes could indicate irritation from something in its environment, low immunity, or perhaps as secondary to something more serious such as trauma to the head that resulted in an eye infection.

Lastly, don't forget to observe how the frogs interact with each other – Red-eyed Tree Frogs are communal frogs, so you will probably be bringing home more than one. Three is a good number, and a ratio of one male to 2-3 females is generally recommended. Try to get frogs that are similar in size so that there will not be a dominant frog in the bunch. You might spend some time observing how they interact with each other before making your final decision.

Chapter Four: Caring for Your New Red-eyed Tree Frog

The biggest investment you will make in caring for and keeping a Red-eyed Tree Frog is their habitat – whether you call it an aquarium, a vivarium, or simply an enclosure. The important thing is to be able to replicate the frog's natural habitat as much as possible in order to make their living conditions optimal, even in captivity. Prepare this at least a week in advance before you even purchase your Red-eyed Tree Frog because it does take some time and tweaking to get it right.

Red-eyed Tree Frogs are arboreal or tree-dwelling frogs that make their homes in forest canopies in dense, tropical forests in southern Mexico and Central America. Vertical and climbing space is therefore important, as well as ideal temperature, humidity and lighting.

Setting up the Red-eyed Tree Frog Habitat

For a standard adult Red-eyed Tree Frog, a 20-38 gallon tank with lots of vertical space is generally considered sufficient, and able to house as many as 3-4 frogs. One standard terrarium of this size is therefore able to support a small community of these communal species. The larger the better is a good rule, especially since you will likely want to add more frogs after some time.

Standard all-glass reptile tanks or terrariums are ideal. They are able to retain heat and humidity, while a secure screen top will allow for proper ventilation and any suitable light fixtures.

Temperature, Lighting and Humidity Requirements

Optimal temperatures for the Red-eyed Tree Frogs range from 78-84 F, without exceeding the mid-80s. At night, this can drop to around 67 degrees, though slightly warmer nighttime temperatures are recommended for smaller or younger frogs.

During the warmer parts of the year, no supplemental heating source may be needed. During the colder months, however, when temperatures begin to drop, low wattage heat bulbs, heating pads, or even red or nocturnal bulbs can provide additional sources of heat that are gentle enough without being excessively drying. Always place artificial heat sources outside the tank – not only does this prevent the frog from accidentally being burned by touching the bulb, it also allows the frog to regulate its own temperature by moving closer or nearer the heat source as it needs.

Unlike with many reptiles, it isn't really necessary to provide lighting for your frogs, but UVB lighting can provide some benefits. These provide needed light for both the frogs and the plants within the tank to ensure optimal growth and development. In addition, some light can help you appreciate these species more by making your viewing easier. Keep any light source on a day/night cycle of at least 14 hours in the summer and eight hours in the winter.

Humidity levels should be kept at moderate to high, with care being taken that the environment does not become soggy or damp. Tropical rainforest environments usually alternative from high humidity to periods of dryness which prevents too much sogginess that can be a breeding ground for bacteria. Too much damp is not good for amphibians because they are extremely susceptible to infections resulting from an unhealthy or contaminated habitat. These alternating periods of dryness and humidity can be replicated by devising a misting schedule which allows the frog's habitat periods of humidity interspersed with periods of necessary dryness.

In general, heavy spraying or misting at least twice daily is sufficient to keep the habitat at humidity levels of 70-90%. Automated misting systems can also be used to maintain the necessary humidity levels even when you are away and unable to mist the cage yourself. An automatic mister or fogger would be suitable. Just make sure that the habitat has adequate ventilation with enough fresh air coming in to prevent the development of any fungus or bacteria.

Keeping Your Red-eyed Tree Frog Happy and Healthy

Be sure to provide a suitably-sized terrarium for your frog to give them sufficient room to explore and move around. In addition, a too-small enclosure can cause unintentional accidents whenever these frogs attempt to leap across the cages and hit the glass walls instead.

Furnish the terrarium with substrate that easily locks in moisture to support ideal humidity levels within the enclosure. Substrate made from coconut husks, orchid bark, leaf litter, and sphagnum moss are ideal, as these are also easy to clean and resistant to mold and fungus.

You will also need to what approximates foliage within the terrarium. This is an arboreal frog and spends much of its time in climbing and hiding within dense canopy, so a lush selection of plant life not only makes your terrarium more attractive, it also makes life more interesting for your frog despite being kept in captivity. Both live and artificial plants can be used together to create as natural an environment for the frogs as possible. Choose plants with large and broad leaves to provide them with sufficient spaces for their occasional needs for shelter, sleeping, and hiding spaces. Be sure to choose plants that will thrive in the recommended temperature and humidity requirements of the tropical environment within the enclosure. Make sure that the plants are free of pesticides and fertilizers by removing it from the soil, rinsing the entire plant including the roots before replanting or repotting it in clean soil. Ensure that all the various things like plants, rocks, substrate and other materials you place in the terrarium is frog-safe by eliminating unnecessary chemicals and substances before putting them in.

Finally, don't forget to equip the enclosure with a large but shallow water dish with fresh and clean water. Being amphibians, these frogs do occasionally swim, even though Red-eyed Tree Frogs prefer to spend most of their time climbing trees. The main advantage of providing a ready source of clean and fresh water is to help maintain the enclosure's humidity levels. If for whatever reason the environment grows too hot for the frogs, these water dishes are excellent retreats for the frogs that may seek out less drying conditions.

If you manage to setup the habitat appropriately, terrarium maintenance need not be a heavy task. Red-eyed Tree Frogs are known for being low maintenance pets, and this includes maintenance concerns. Spot cleaning at least once a week or when necessary is sufficient, with more extensive cleaning whenever the need arises – though generally this can be done some once or twice a year as a general average for a terrarium that houses 1-2 frogs. The leaves of plants can be wiped when needed, and the substrate changed once in a while as long as it does not sit in water. The water should, however, be changed daily to prevent dirty and contaminated water that might result in infections. Regular cleaning such as wiping the glass and removing the frog's waste can go a long way to maintaining your frog's health and longevity.

Chapter Five: Feeding Your Red-eyed Tree Frog

Like most frogs, Red-eyed Tree Frogs are mainly insectivores, which means that you will need to feed them live prey such as insects and other invertebrates. Expect to be handling (and feeding) live prey, because some frogs won't even consider eating food that isn't moving. If you are a squeamish person who balks at the thought of this, then perhaps a pet frog is not for you.

Aside from providing your frog with an appropriate habitat, making sure that they are fed well is the other important thing you have to do to make sure that your frogs thrive. There may be some difficulty at first, especially if your frog is still adjusting to its new environment and is still hesitant about feeding, but if your frog is healthy and in good condition, its appetite will naturally take its course and you'll find it feeding quite well.

In the wild, the Red-eyed Tree frog sits and waits for its prey. Using its sense of sight and smell, it waits for prey to come into striking distance. Once it does, it flips out its sticky tongue and then retracts it to pull the prey back into its mouth. It can be pretty interesting to observe just how long and sticky its tongue can be when it is hunting. It is particularly fascinating to watch just how fast they can use their tongue to catch their food. This species does have teeth, but are mostly used for holding onto the prey, and the food is almost always swallowed whole.

The Basics of a Red-eyed Tree Frog's Diet

A Red-eyed Tree Frog's diet in captivity mainly consists of crickets since these are readily available – you can find them easily in pet shops, or you can raise them yourself. In the wild, these species have also been known to feed on other worms and insects such as beetles, grasshoppers, flies and moths.

It is important to feed your frog appropriately-sized food – ideally smaller than the head of your frog so that they can easily swallow and digest the prey. If you are feeding them smaller insects, then simply increase the portions accordingly.

Remember that this is a nocturnal species, so they will be feeding mainly at night.

Gut Loading Crickets

"Gut loading" the crickets before actually feeding them to your frogs is often done to ensure that your frog gets the necessary nutrients and vitamins that it needs – despite the lack of variety in its diet if you are feeding it mainly on crickets alone. This is done by feeding the crickets or "loading" them to ensure that your frog is getting all the nutrients it needs. There are a number of cricket diets available, and you can feed them at least 24 hours before offering them to your frog.

Another way of ensuring your frog's good health is to "dust" the crickets with calcium powder, vitamin D3, and a multivitamin supplement. You do this by placing the crickets in a bag together with the vitamin or calcium product, and shaking the bag gives the crickets a good coating of the said product. This supplement is especially important for the smaller frogs that still have a lot of growing to do.

Tips for Feeding Your Red-eyed Tree Frog

Feeding times can be done every other day, with a meal size of about 3-4 crickets per feeding. For juveniles, however, feeding should be more frequent as they need more nutrition to help their growth and development.

To feed your Red-eyed Tree Frog, simply throw in some 3-4 crickets (depending on how many frogs you are keeping) into their tank every other day. They will eat if they are hungry, and will simply ignore the food if they are not hungry. Uneaten food that dies in the cage should be removed – frogs usually only eat moving food, and any dead insects within the enclosure may eventually contribute to the growth of bacteria or fungus inside the enclosure.

While some keepers simply throw the prey into the cage and trust that their frogs' instincts will lead it to catch the food, others prefer to use a feeder, which is basically a container from which the food will not be able to escape. Either method is feasible as long as your frog is able to feed well. Using a feeder, however, can keep the crickets from escaping – especially if your frog's tank is topped by a locking screen.

While they are still tadpoles, they will feed primarily on algae. It is after they have grown in size metamorphosed into frogs that they begin to feed on insects such as small or flightless fruit flies and pinhead crickets.

Tiny frogs whose hunting instincts are still not well-developed can be given flightless fruitflies or bloodworms. As they grow into juveniles, they can eventually transition to crickets. Again, remember that food you give them should be selected carefully based on size, and should, in no instance, be larger than your frog's head. It is true that some have been known to eat smaller frogs and even other reptiles or lizards, but on the whole they prefer smaller prey that can be easily swallowed.

While some frogs will simply ignore food when it is not hungry, there are some that have been known to overfeed. This is unhealthy, and even dangerous to frogs as they can literally eat themselves to death. On the other hand, frogs that are not eating could be a symptom of some other serious illness. Try to provide them a little variety in their food by offering them other insects, or moving insects if so far what you have been giving them are unmoving prey. If they still refuse to eat, bring them to a veterinarian to determine if their lack of appetite may be a symptom of an illness or disease.

Finally, don't forget to keep your frog's habitat well supplied with clean and fresh water. Changing their water daily prevents them from drinking or soaking in dirty or contaminated water.

Chapter Six: The Life Cycle of a Red-eyed Tree Frog

It is always an educational experience to care for a Red-eyed Tree Frog. Even if their nocturnal lifestyles make watching them during the day a bit boring, watching them hatch from their eggs and then grow and metamorphose into their adult selves is a fascinating journey – of how a creature can evolve and move from water, to land, and eventually to the tops of trees.

As with the traditional definition of amphibians, frogs can live in both land and water. But to be more precise about it, frogs as amphibians are unique in starting out their lives living in water and eventually metamorphose from tadpoles with gills to adults with lungs. The permeable skin of amphibians also function as secondary respiratory surfaces. 90% of known amphibian species today comprise of frogs.

Breeding and Reproduction

This arboreal frog species spends much of its time high up in tree canopies and foliage, but they do come down during the mating season. They gravitate towards ground pools in order to breed. This is the reason why they generally spend their lives near water – eventually, it is to the water that they must go if they are to reproduce.

The Red-eyed Tree Frog's breeding season occurs during the summer months. Following heavy rains, the males have a distinct call which they use to signify to the females their readiness to mate, as well as to establish their territory. Male frogs have also been known to shake the branches in order to keep rivals at bay and therefore improve their chances of finding a mate.

Amplexus, which is a kind of restraining embrace, happens when the female carries the male on its back while "oviposition" takes place. Oviposition is the process whereby the female chooses a spot above water and lays a clutch or clutches of eggs. As the male grasps the female with his forelimbs, they remain in amplexus with their cloaca positioned close together. The female lays the eggs and the male covers them with sperm, thus the eggs are fertilized externally.

The pair positions themselves on leaves above water, and it is on these leaves that the female deposits its eggs. The males fertilize the eggs as they are deposited by the females. A kind of sticky jelly is also produced not only to protect the eggs but also to hold the eggs together and in position.

The Eggs or Frogspawn

The choice of location for egg laying is to enable the small tadpoles to fall directly into water after they hatch. The eggs of a Red-eyed Tree Frog are white and small, and start out encased in a jelly-like substance which protects them until they hatch some 5-9 days later. When the eggs hatch, the tadpoles that emerge fall directly into the water below, where they begin swimming using their tail. These larvae are initially adapted solely to an aquatic lifestyle.

When several eggs are clumped together, this is known collectively as frogspawn. Interestingly, larvae are able to detect vibrations caused by nearby predators, and as a matter of protection – and to avoid being eaten – the eggs will actually hatch earlier than usual. This is known as phenotypic plasticity, where eggs or embryos hatch early as a manner of self-protection.

Larvae or Tadpoles

The tiny brown tadpoles are much like fish because they breathe using gills and swim aided by a tail. This part or phase of their life usually lasts from 7-9 weeks.

As the tadpoles grow, they begin to develop legs which enable them to crawl out of the water and towards land. What takes place next is known as apoptosis, a kind of controlled cell death which results in the reabsorption of the organs that have become redundant. Thus, the frog's tail begins to shrink until it has been fully absorbed. Eventually, the lungs develop and the gills and gill pouch eventually disappear even as the legs appear, as they metamorphose into froglets or tiny frogs, which they must do before the pools dry out. As metamorphosis continues, eyes are repositioned and eyelids are formed, and legs, a large jaw, and a tongue is formed. The skin also becomes thicker and tougher. When the tail is gone, the tiny new frog can begin to live its life out of the water, moving into hiding places in the plants near the pool until it can eventually use its feet and the powerful suction cups on their toes to leap and climb higher up into the trees.

Froglets or Young Frogs

The Red-eyed Tree Frogs start out their young frog lives quite different in coloring from their adult selves. They are usually of a mustard color when young, and their distinctive and vivid coloring of bright red eyes against a general green coloring, blue and yellow sides and orange toes only come as they mature.

Adult Frogs

The adult Red-eyed Tree Frog has large and bulging brightly colored red eyes. The sides are striped with blue and yellow stripes, the feed are red-orange, the upper legs are blue, and the body is an overall bright green color.

Females generally range in size of about 3 inches long, while the males are slightly smaller at 2 inches. Sexual maturity is reached at around 3-4 years, uring which after which the cycle starts again.

Chapter Seven: Red-eyed Tree Frog Temperament, Handling, and Behavioral Adaptations

If you have made it this far in this book, then it seems obvious that Red-eyed Tree Frogs are not especially difficult pets to care for, but that they do require a specialized kind of care. Try to do as much species-specific research as possible, before you bring your frog home, and during the course of your care of your Red-eyed Tree Frog. Not all amphibians will require the same kind of care, and the same goes for the different species of frogs and toads. Don't assume anything – check your facts and verify details. Too often, frogs that die in captivity do so because of inaccurate information and poor husbandry practices.

Temperament and Handling

These attractive and vividly colored frogs have grown steadily in popularity among keepers and hobbyists not only because of how they look, or because they are comparatively easy to obtain. In terms of temperament, Red-eyed Tree Frogs are also calm and placid, and are not given to undue aggression or biting.

They can become a bit boring to watch – being nocturnal creatures, their periods of great activity are during the night, and while they do occasionally wake up during the day to feed, they are quiet most of the time. An exception to this is during the breeding season when they can become quite noisy with their mating calls, particularly the males.

Red-eyed Tree Frogs are not solitary creatures, and they will thrive more in a small community of their own species than when alone. In general, an average of 3-4 Red-eyes, with a general ratio of 1 male to 2-3 females is a good communal setup. This reduces territoriality among the males while providing sufficient socialization opportunities so that your frog does not get lonely.

But just because they are social with their own kind does not mean they will appreciate being social with you. Red-eyed Tree Frogs, just like most frog species, do not appreciate being handled, and this is not something they are likely to get used to even with time. This is a beautiful species of frogs, and admiring and observing them from behind the glass walls of their enclosures should be sufficient. If they are subjected to excessive handling, this can cause them stress that can eventually lead to illness and even death.

If for whatever reason you do find that it becomes necessary to handle your Red- eyed Tree Frog, always keep these handling times brief, and w so with proper caution. Be gentle, never shake them, and always handle them with wet hands so that their skin's protective mucus is not removed. Always remember that amphibian skin is permeable and can absorb substances and nutrients from the environment, so your hands should always be free of soap, cream, alcohol, and other chemical substances. Needless to say, wash your hands well after handling your frog. Their skin secretions may also cause irritation, especially when it gets into the eyes, mouth, or even wounds. And frogs do sometimes carry diseases like Salmonella which can be passed on to humans.

Adaptation Behavior and Defenses

It isn't just the Red-eyed Tree Frog's life cycle that makes them such fascinating and educational creatures to keep, but there are also the various specialized behavioral adaptations and defense mechanisms that they use to survive and thrive in their natural environment.

Climbing Ability

Being mainly arboreal, the Red-eyed Tree Frog is an excellent jumper and can jump up to twenty times its length. They are also well-equipped to move from tree to tree and even to cling to the undersides of trees. Their bright orange feet have a kind of suction that provides them with a very firm and amazing grip even when upside down. This grip also enables the males to hold on to and restrain the female during amplexus, which he can do for several hours as the eggs are laid by the female and fertilized by the male.

Ectothermic and Hibernation

Frogs in general, including the Red-eyed Tree Frog, are ectotherms, or "cold-blooded," which means that they rely on their environment to regulate their body temperature. Because they cannot regulate their temperature internally, they rely on environmental conditions to do this for them. Thus, they will "bask" in the sun when they need to raise their temperatures, or they will move to a shelter and away from sunlight if they are beginning to overheat. Other frog behavior which helps them thermoregulate are by drawing heat from the environment such as by sunning themselves upon rocks, entering the water to cool down, or make use of evaporative cooling – which is when water evaporates from the frog's skin, creating a cooling effect. During the winter time, on the other hand, they are able to protect themselves and to survive by hibernating.

Hibernating involves the creation of a hibernaculum, or a space in which they will be safe and protected from both predators and the weather. Then when the frog begins to settle in to sleep through the winter, its metabolism slows down, enabling it to survive for long periods even without eating. After winter passes and springtime arrives, the frog wakes up and what is usually first on its mind is mating and feeding.

This is one of the reasons why breeders attempt to replicate "winter-like-conditions," or at least begins to lower the habitat's temperatures to lower than normal. In the wild or in natural conditions, mating and breeding season takes place during springtime, which follows closely after winter and periods of long hibernation.

Calling

While mainly a quiet species, the Red-eyed Tree Frog can also be quite vocal during breeding season. They do this by passing air through the larynx, and then sound is subsequently amplified by the vocal sacs or the skin membranes underneath their throat. Most of their calls are actually made with their mouths closed – when the vocal sacs are filled with air, they can call continuously, even under water.

While most calls are made by the males in order to attract a mate during breeding season, this species also has a range of other calls. Females call to signify that her eggs are ready and that she is also ready to mate. Some males will make a different kind of call when involved in a territorial dispute with another male, or simply to warn off other males to stay away from the territory they have marked out. Sometimes, a distress call can also be made in times of danger, which is perhaps the only call this frog makes with its mouth open, producing a higher-pitched call. In addition to their startle coloration defense mechanism, this call is intended to distract the predator long enough so that the frog has time to escape.

Camouflage

While there are frog species that defend themselves through poison or toxins, the poisonless Red-eyed Tree Frog relies more on careful and subtle manipulation of its colouring to protect and defend itself.

During the daytime, for instance, when the frog is basically inactive, it protects itself by remaining motionless and hiding its blue and yellow coloring with its back legs. When they close their eyes and tuck their orange feet underneath their bellies, they look almost completely green and become indistinguishable against the green leaves and foliage of the trees, thus protecting themselves by essentially hiding in plain sight.

Nictitating Membrane

Red-eyed Tree Frogs have a third eyelid in addition to their upper and lower eyelids. This third eyelid is called the nictitating membrane, and serves to cover the eye completely. This is a semitransparent membrane that not only allows the frog to see underwater, but also allows it to hide from predators by concealing their bright red eyes when they are asleep or simply wish to hide.

But really, this third membrane has a lot more uses – they also use it to protect their eyes and to keep moisture in. They can close their third eyelid only halfway – allowing them to see more clearly than if it were fully closed, while at the same time offering a measure of protection – whether it be against predators, the water when they are swimming, or environmental elements such as wind or drying heat.

While it does limit their eyesight when fully closed, it is still transparent which still allows them to see partially. If they wish to swim, for instance, they can rely on their sense of smell to guide them when their limited vision is not enough.

Deimatic Behavior

Another way that the Red-eyed Tree Frog uses its unique coloring to protect itself is by deimatic behavior or "startle coloration" which essentially consists of sudden displays of their vivid colors to approaching predators. By suddenly staring at the predator with the bright red eyes for which this frog is named, and also suddenly unfurling its legs all its vivid colors in a quick flash, the predator is momentarily distracted, startled, or even scared , thus giving the frog a chance to flee or escape. Often the startling and shocking colors can also create a ghost image that confuses the predator as the frog makes its escape.

Phenotypic Plasticity

Phenotypic plasticity is manifested by the embryos of Red-eyed Tree Frogs. In response to vibrations created by approaching predators or environmental changes that can signal a threatening rainstorm, the embryos will hatch early in order to protect themselves. Essentially, they are now enabled to fall into the water and escape by swimming away. This is true despite a normal hatching period of 6-10 days from being laid. Interestingly, it seems that even when the embryos are in their eggs, they are fully capable of assessing potential threats in their environment since it has been found that other types of vibrations or disturbances, when unthreatening, do not actually cause early hatching.

Chapter Eight: Breeding Your Red-eyed Tree Frog

The breeding of Red-eyed Tree Frogs is pretty straightforward and can often be one of the most rewarding experiences for a hobbyist or enthusiast. In fact, many breeders recommend captive breeding not only to decrease the chances of wild caught Red-eyed Tree Frogs being sold in the pet trade, but also because of the prevalent fungal infection infecting worldwide amphibian species, and which have already drastically reduced the numbers of frog and amphibian species worldwide. Captive breeding reduces the risk of infected wild caught frogs passing on this disease to otherwise healthy captive Red-eyed Tree Frogs.

While you can certainly breed from a pair of Red-eyed Tree Frogs, most breeders have noted greater success in their breeding attempts when it involves multiple males and females. The optimal ratio of male to female is three or more males to two or more females for successful breeding. Needless to say, your selected breeding frogs should be in good health and of a mature age and sexually mature. Breeding in captivity is done through a careful manipulation of the frogs' environment to approximate seasonal changes in their natural environment which also induces mating and reproductive behavior. A frog in poor condition may not do well under these environmental changes, nor can their fertility be assured. In general, mature males are around 2 to 2.5 inches in length, while females mature at just under 3 inches.

Basic Red-eyed Tree Frog Breeding Information

The breeding season of Red-eyed Tree Frogs usually occurs during the rainy season, or from late May through November, with peak seasons occurring in June. Occasionally, a second peak can occur again in October.

This can be induced artificially in captivity which means that Red-eyed Tree Frogs can breed year-round, but breeding attempts are apparently more successful if they are timed to coincide with the frog's natural breeding season out in the wild. Of course, even if you are timing the breeding of your frogs with nature's seasons, the "rainy season" will still have to be created artificially within your frog's artificial habitat – and for this purpose, you will need to create a Rain Chamber.

Preparing your frogs for breeding requires some one to three months of heavy feeding and being kept in relatively dry conditions. This is a way of approximating natural seasonal changes of a dry season followed by a wet season – the latter mimicking spring and the Red-eyed Tree Frog's natural breeding season. Don't forget to provide your frog with a ready supply of fresh water, however, even when you are simulating a dry season. The misting of the terrarium can be cut down to twice a week, and during this time, the frogs' food intake can be increased by around 25%. The humidity should be lowered to 30 or 40, and the temperatures lowered to 73F during the day, and 65 F during the night.

After a month or about 30 days and a week or two before the planned breeding attempt, return temperatures and feeding quantities to normal, and begin to mist heavily at least twice a day. The frogs will signal their readiness to mate when the males start vocalizing or calling. This is his way of calling to the female. The females, on the other hand, will look swollen – this is a sign that the eggs are developing.

Setting up the Rain Chamber

The Rain Chamber is group housing for Red-eyed Tree Frogs for breeding purposes and approximates a jungle environment during a rainstorm. Because this species thrives in groups or communities, housing them together should present no great challenges in terms of acclimatization. A Rain Chamber is any waterproof container that is equipped with a spray connected to a pump at the top. Turning on the pump simulates a rainstorm, and this should be allowed to run for some three to four hours around dusk until night. Using an electrical timer can simplify this process considerably.

The Rain Chamber should also be equipped with several tropical plants with broad leaves – for Red-eyed Tree Frogs, amplexus, as well as egg laying, usually takes place on the underside of leaves overhanging water. The plants can be set up in ceramic pots or bark slabs, though it is advisable to pick a plant that grows well in water without soil since this will enable you to set up the plant right atop the water, while the plant's roots will also provide the frogs with climbing space and keep them from drowning. Also, a large and lush plant will not only enhance aesthetics within the Rain Chamber, it will also provide the frogs a more interesting environment with roots and branches and leaves to crawl onto, perch, and climb over.

Keep temperatures within the Rain Chamber at around 80 degrees, and remember to keep the water level at shallow enough levels to prevent any occurrences of accidental drowning. Also ensure that the Rain Chamber has sufficient ventilation. Rain-tree Frogs are not completely aquatic, and will still need adequate ventilation. Place this somewhere with sufficient natural light, but out of direct sunlight.

Within one to two days or whenever the frogs are ready, amplexus occurs. Amplexus usually takes place underneath leaves overhanging water, and transpires when the male climbs onto the female's back and grasps her under the front legs. He will remain in this position until the female frog lays eggs. Once she does, he deposits his sperm over the eggs. They will not be feeding during this time or any time during their stay within the rain chamber – this is why it is important to make sure that they have been fed well beforehand.

Amplexus can last anywhere from one to several days to a week. They will separate naturally whenever they are ready – or until the female begins to lay her eggs.

The female may deposit eggs in 3-4 clusters, with each cluster containing anywhere from a few to almost 70 eggs, with an average range of 20-40 eggs. These eggs should be incubated at around 75 F.

Once the eggs have been laid and fertilized, you should remove the leaves containing the eggs because it is not unheard of for the breeding pair to feed on the eggs and the young. Many breeders, however, take the leaves with the eggs underneath, and suspend these over frog-safe water contained in a glass. Occasionally, a plastic slide or tube is provided to facilitate the tadpoles' descent into the water below. The eggs themselves are clear, and one can clearly see the developing embryos wriggling within.

On the average, tadpoles will hatch from the eggs 10-14 days after being laid, though occasionally they can take as long as 21 days, and drop or slide directly into the water underneath the leaves. After 3-4 days, the tadpoles will be actively swimming in the water.

Tips for Breeding Red-eyed Tree Frogs

- The reason why most breeders recommend a higher ratio of frogs than a simple breeding pair is because competition seems to encourage breeding. More males than females can lead the males to be more energetic in their reproductive behavior, thus increasing the odds of a successful breeding.

- Frogs are said to be sensitive to barometric pressure, so even when you are artificially creating rainy conditions within their enclosure, you might want to wait until it an actual storm front before moving your frogs into the Rain Chamber as this has been said to increase the chances of successful mating. However, Red-eyed Tree Frogs can certainly be potentially bred year-round.

- Throughout the preparation for breeding and the breeding process itself, up to the laying of the eggs and the hatching of the eggs, part of the water in the container should always be changed daily. This prevents the accumulation of waste in the water that may eventually cause illness or disease in the frogs or the eggs and tadpoles.

- Sometimes, the female will also lay eggs on the side of the Rain Chamber. This is okay as long as the eggs are still located above water. While some breeders remove the leaves and move the eggs to a different container, others simply remove the adults and leave the eggs in the Rain Chamber. The important thing is to separate the adults from the eggs after they have been laid. This is to prevent the adults from feeding on or climbing on the leaves, damaging, or dislodging the eggs. Should the eggs be knocked into the water, these will certainly drown.

- Should the female lay her eggs successively on different nights, you might want to cut each leaf off and remove them to a different container after the eggs are laid. Just make sure to position the leaves and the eggs securely over water.
- The metamorphosed tadpoles are quite capable of scaling the sides of the aquarium using their new legs, so make sure that the top is secured with a screen top. You might also want to provide them with a place to climb onto after their legs have developed. Floating driftwood or cork bark often works well.

Raising Red-eyed Tree Frog Tadpoles

Tadpoles should be allowed sufficient housing because a too-tight space can induce them to be cannibalistic. 20-30 tadpoles kept in 2-3 inches of water per 5 gallon tub is a good starting point, though the number of tadpoles per tub should be reduced as the tadpoles begin to grow in size.

Half of the water should be replaced with fresh water at least twice a week, but the frequency should be increased to every other day when the tadpoles begin to grow. Also remove daily any visible waste and uneaten food.

Feed the tadpoles daily with finely crushed fish food, or brine shrimp flakes. Food can often be consumed within as little as 10 minutes.

Tadpole development and metamorphosis can proceed at different rates, but often takes a month to two months. In general, rear legs become apparent at 30 days, and front legs in 36 days. Once the front legs have appeared, the tadpoles will begin to climb out of the water even if they have not yet fully reabsorbed their tails. Some will actually climb up the walls of the terrarium so be sure that the enclosure is securely locked at the top. You may wish to provide a place where the young frogs can climb onto after their legs have appeared – a large rock, a pile of gravel, or even floating driftwood.

The froglets will usually stop eating until after they have reabsorbed their tail completely, so don't worry if you notice that they aren't feeding anymore. After they have climbed out of the water, they will usually just sit still until they have absorbed their tail. Essentially, the frog will be "feeding" on their tail for several days. When their tails are gone, you can resume feeding them, ideally offering them flightless fruit flies or small crickets. By this time, they can be housed just like adults, though in smaller tanks corresponding to their size. Make sure that their enclosure stays moist because baby frogs can often be prone to drying.

Chapter Nine: Keeping Your Red-Eyed Tree Frog Healthy

As with the keeping of most exotic pets, you should be aware that it may not always be easy to find a veterinarian in your area that has sufficient knowledge and experience in dealing with exotic pets such as frogs and other amphibians.

Prevention is always better than a cure. Many of the health conditions that can afflict Red-eyed Tree Frogs stem from inappropriate environmental conditions and poor husbandry. Knowledge, is therefore your first means of combating potential illnesses in your pet frog. What kind of habitat is best for your frog? What about their diet? Exercise? What possible signs should you be on the lookout for that might tell you that your frog is ill?

You should therefore educate yourself as much as you can about these beautiful creatures, their normal behavior, as well as their appearance. After learning as much as you can about the Red-eyed Tree Frogs, you should be able to recognize when something is different or when your frog is showing outward behavior or signs that its health may be compromised. Your observational skill and your knowledge are ultimately your frog's first line of defense against illness of any kind, and this is particularly true if you haven't found a veterinary specialist with enough experience dealing with frogs and other amphibians.

One of the leading causes of illnesses or untimely death among some Red-eyed Tree Frogs being kept in captivity is often simply poor husbandry, which stems from lack of, or possession of inaccurate, knowledge and information. For instance, it is not advisable to handle your frog unless it is absolutely necessary. This is not only because of the stress that being handled may cause them, but also because frogs are capable of absorbing substances through their skin, and the human hand may sometimes contain oils that are toxic to frogs.

And finally, in no case should frogs be transported without the proper permits or licenses – certain infectious diseases that afflict frogs, such as chytridiomycosis, or Chytrid Fungus, are transmittable and contagious, and have already dramatically reduced frog populations all over the world.

Common Conditions Affecting Red-eyed Tree Frogs

Some of the more common conditions that Red-eyed Tree Frogs can suffer from include:

- Oodinium
- Red Leg Disease
- Metabolic Bone Disease
- Chytrid Fungus

Oodinium

Common among red-eyed tree frogs in captivity is Oodinium. This is a kind of fungal infection that in frogs originating from warmer climates such as the Red-eyed Tree Frog, can manifest as small whitish, gray, or yellow and velvety spots that appear over the frog's skin.

This is commonly caused by dirty or unsanitary habitats, though is naturally also attributable to the natural moist environment of their habitat. It is therefore important that the frog's enclosure be cleaned and maintained regularly.

Treatment generally depends on the cause – so it is always advisable to consult first with your veterinarian. If an unhealthy environment is the root of the infection, then one can usually treat this condition by placing the frog in distilled water and then thoroughly cleaning their habitat. If this does not work, please bring your frog to a vet immediately.

Fungal infections in certain species of frogs can be quite lethal – as it would seem that the immune system of frogs are not very resistant to this kind of infections. In recent years, fungal infections have caused the severe decrease of various frog populations throughout the world and should therefore not be taken lightly.

Perhaps the best way to keep your Red-eyed tree frog in optimal condition is to learn as much as you can about it. In general, this is a species that does not tolerate well inadequate or inappropriate surroundings. You can single-handedly cause ill health or even death in your frog by giving them the wrong type of environment.

Red Leg Disease

This is perhaps the most well-known health condition among frogs, and is more of a syndrome rather than an actual disease. This condition is caused by septicaemia due to various bacteria including the Pseudomonas Aeruginosa, Proteus Mirabilis and Aeromonas Hydrophyla.

The classic reddening of the abdomen and legs for which this condition is named is the result of the pooling of blood under the frog's skin – generally the result of ruptured blood vessels or hemorrhaging. Other possible symptoms include hematomas, inactivity, swelling, fluid accumulation in the abdomen, open sores that don't heal, and a general sluggishness or apathy in the frog. Clogged veins may be present, and in very severe cases, blood poisoning may occur. When this happens, the disease can become fatal and result in convulsions and unexpected death. Of course, when the disease does reach this level of severity, its progress is usually quite rapid.

Red Leg Disease results from various causes such as parasites from unclean environmental conditions, stress caused by inappropriate living conditions, overcrowding, improper handling, contaminated food, unclean water and exposure to toxic substances such as pesticides. Check the lighting, humidity, temperature, and overall cleanliness of your frog's environment – warning should be given here that red leg disease can be highly contagious, so if you suspect your frog of having it, they should be immediately isolated and given immediate treatment. Minimize unnecessary handling as much as possible.

Treatment may consist of an antibacterial bath, antibacterial medication, and dietary control, though this is by no means a cure. Please consult with your veterinarian for the best way of treating your Red-eyed Tree Frog. Unfortunately, because of the rapid progress of this disease, prognosis is usually poor, and mortality rates high.

Metabolic Bone Disease (MBD)

Metabolic Bone Disease (MBD) is another common condition among Red-eyed Tree Frogs in captivity. This is a condition caused by calcium, vitamin D3, and phosphorous deficiency, or sometimes by a calcium metabolism disorder in which the frog is unable to process calcium immediately. Symptoms to watch out for include swollen legs, receded lower jaw, constipation, weakness, or a softening or swelling of the jaw. As the condition progresses, there can be lethargy, loss of appetite, and an inability or unwillingness to jump. This can be quite a serious problem, and the resulting weakened bones may result in distorted or crippled limbs. Hopping may sometimes even cause their bones to break.

Treatment is generally by supplementing their diet with calcium – either by feeding supplement pellets to crickets, or dusting the crickets with calcium or multivitamin powder. This is particularly important if you are keeping your frog on an exclusive cricket diet (which are often the easiest to obtain) – as crickets are not precisely good sources of calcium.

The good news is that if caught early, MBD is treatable or reversible. But because some of the earlier symptoms are quite subtle, it may not be an easy condition to catch in its earlier stage. It is recommended that you prevent MBD from occurring in the first place by providing a properly balanced diet, complete with calcium, vitamins, and other nutrients. Proper lighting (UV-B lighting) and temperature, light and dark cycles, and sufficient room for exercise is also recommended. Needless to say, you should consult your veterinarian regarding diagnosis of MBD and possible treatments.

Chytrid Fungus

The Chytrid Fungus, or chytridiomycosis, also called the *Batrachochytrium dendrobatidis* is a fungal disease that is considered a threat not only to Red-eyed Tree Frogs, but to many species of frogs and other amphibians all over the world. It has been found to occur in all continents except

Antarctica, and have caused a serious decline in amphibian populations with the most dramatic mortalities documented in Australia, Central America, and North America. Overall, this disease has been credited with over 100 species extinctions since the 70's.

This disease begins by attacking the frog's skin before moving towards the internal organs. Thus, many of the initial symptoms will be noticeable on keratin-containing layers of the skin, including discoloration, peeling of the outside layers, thickening of the skin, and a general roughness of the skin. The result is that the animal has difficulty breathing, and is unable to properly regulate electrolytes, often leading to a heart attack.

Once the condition starts moving internally, symptoms will also include loss of appetite, lethargy or sluggishness, and seizures. The hind legs might be spread out, and the frog unable to right itself.

If the frog contracts the fungus during its tadpole stage, when they can pick up the chytrid spores from the water, the subsequent metamorphosis that the tadpole undergoes spreads the fungus because the frog's immune system is suppressed during this transitional stage. As a result, the fungus is allowed to spread and becomes more aggressive.

If suspected, the infected frog should be isolated and kept in quarantine. This is an aquatic fungus and while its precise method of transmission is not precisely known, it is contagious or transmissible and so other frogs and amphibians in the immediate environment are likely to also be affected. If the intensity of the infection spreads, death results. This is a fatal disease and has already killed a number of frog populations in the wild, though if caught early, treatment efforts may still be successful.

If your frog should die from the disease, please refrain from touching the frog directly with your hands. Use gloves in handling the frog as well as anything it may have come into contact with in its environment, including its water, in order to prevent its spread to other areas. One of the best ways to prevent this disease in the first place is to avoid purchasing wild caught frogs, and to purchase only Red-eyed Tree Frogs that were raised in captivity. At present, treatment options include anti-fungal medication and heat-induced therapy. These have worked well in some frog species, but not so well in others.

Red-eyed Tree Frog Care Sheet

We summarize the essentials of the information presented in the rest of this book in this final section. It allows you to see at a glance what kind of pet a Red-eyed Tree Frog would make, and what caring for and keeping one entails. Even if you don't have the time to read through this entire book, this last section pretty much summarizes all the pertinent information regarding this beautiful and very popular frog breed – from life cycles, breeding, feeding, behavior, housing, and possible health concerns.

1.) Basic Red-eyed Tree Frog Information

Scientific Name: Agalychnis callidryas

Kingdom: Animalia

Phylum: Chordata

Class: Amphibia

Order: Anura

Family: Hylidae

Genus: Agalychnis

Species: A. callidryas

Regions of Origin: Southern Mexico, Central America, northern South America, including southern Veracruz, Oaxaca in Mexico, central and eastern Panama, northern Colombia, southwestern Nicaragua, and southwestern Costa Rica

Primary Habitat: Near rivers and ponds in rainforests, humid and tropical lowlands

Description: The body is primarily a vibrant green color, with yellow and blue vertical stripes; it has webbed feet and toes which are orange/red. As per its name, it has red eyes with vertical narrow pupils.

Primary Behavioral Characteristics: Nocturnal, communal frogs, arboreal, and carnivorous

Health Conditions: Oodinium, Red Leg Disease, Metabolic Bone Disease, Chytrid Fungus

Lifespan: average of 5 years, but may live longer

2.) Habitat Requirements

Recommended Equipment: standard 20 gallon tank or terrarium secured with a screen top, and equipped with substrate, water dish, and climbing and hiding structures such as branches, artificial or natural plants with broad leaves

Recommended Temperature: 78-84 F

Recommended Humidity Level: 80-90%

Cleaning Frequency: Spot cleaning daily, with a more thorough cleaning at least once every 4-6 months, or more frequently if necessary

3.) Feeding and Diet

Primary Diet: Crickets, moths, flies and other insects, and sometimes a variety of worms

Feeding Frequency (tadpoles): Feed 2-3 times a week

Feeding Frequency (juvenile): Feed daily or up to 4 times a week

Feeding Frequency (adult): Every 2-3 days

Water: Clean water in a water dish should always be freely available

4.) Breeding Information

Age of Sexual Maturity: Sexual maturity is reached at around 2 years, but breeding can take place at around 3-4 years

Incubation Period: 6-7 days

Metamorphosis: Can around 36 or more days

Clutch Size: roughly 30-50, or an average of 40 eggs

Average Adult Size: 2-3 inches, with females being larger than the males

Index

Photo Credits

Page 1 Photo by Tim Ross via Wikimedia Commons. <https://commons.wikimedia.org/wiki/File:03-04RedEyedFrog.jpg>

Page 7 Photo by Miquel Adroer via Wikimedia Commons. <https://commons.wikimedia.org/wiki/File:Granota_ulls_vermells.jpg>

Page 13 Photo by Carey James Balboa via Wikimedia Commons. <https://commons.wikimedia.org/wiki/File:Red_eyed_tree_frog.jpg>

Page 25 Photo by Geoff Gallice via Wikimedia Commons. <https://commons.wikimedia.org/wiki/File:Red-eyed_Tree_Frog_(Agalychnis_callidryas)_3.jpg>

Page 31 Photo by Thomas Shahan via Wikimedia Commons. <https://commons.wikimedia.org/wiki/File:Red-Eyed_Tree_Frog_(Agalychnis_sp.)_-_Belize.jpg>

Page 37 Photo by katja via Pixabay. <https://pixabay.com/en/frog-red-eyed-tree-frog-jungle-1434425/>

Page 43 Photo by Frank Vassen via Wikimedia Commons. <https://commons.wikimedia.org/wiki/File:Red-eyed_Tree-

frog,_Esquinas_Rainforest_Lodge,_Costa_Rica_(397650090
9).jpg>

Page 49 Photo by skeeze via Pixabay.
<https://pixabay.com/en/frog-red-eyed-tree-amphibian-
647765/>

Page 59 Photo by Brian Gatwicke via Wikimedia Commons.
<https://commons.wikimedia.org/wiki/File:Red_eyed_tree_
frog_amplexant_pair.jpg>

Page 69 Photo by Esztom via Wikimedia Commons.
<https://commons.wikimedia.org/wiki/File:Agalychnis.jpg
>

Page 79 Photo by Bernard DUPONT via Wikimedia
Commons.
<https://commons.wikimedia.org/wiki/File:Red-
eyed_Tree_Frog_(Agalychnis_callidryas)_(6941089388).jpg
>

References

"11 Colorful Facts About the Red-Eyed Tree Frog." Rebecca OConnell. <http://mentalfloss.com/article/63622/11-colorful-facts-about-red-eyed-tree-frog>

"A Highly Vocal Amphibian: Red Eyed Tree Frog Calling." Red Eyed Tree Frog. <http://www.redeyedtreefrog.org/highly-vocal-amphibian-red-eyed-tree-frog-calling/>

"About Tree Frogs." Andrea Gust. <https://www.treefrog.ca/red-eyed-tree-frog>

"Agalychnis callidryas." amphibiaweb. <http://www.amphibiaweb.org/cgi/amphib_query?where-scientific_name=callidryas>

"Agalychnis callidryas." Wikipedia. <https://en.wikipedia.org/wiki/Agalychnis_callidryas>

"Amphibian." Wikipedia. <https://en.wikipedia.org/wiki/Amphibian>

"Amphibian Red Leg Disease: Causes, Signs, Diagnosis, Treatment, and Prevention." Pet Education. <https://en.wikivet.net/Red-leg_Syndrome>

"An Overview of Chytridiomycosis." Kellie Whittaker and Vance Vredenburg. <http://amphibiaweb.org/chytrid/chytridiomycosis.html>

"Behavioral Characteristics." Red Eyed Tree Frog. <http://www.redeyedtreefrog.org/behavioral-characteristics/>

"Breeding Red-Eyed Treefrogs." Devin Edmonds. <http://www.reptilesmagazine.com/Reptile-Magazines/Reptiles-Magazine/August-2011/Red-Eyed-Treefrog-Rain-Chamber/>

"Breeding Red-Eyed Treefrogs." Eileen Underwood, PhD. <http://www.reptilesmagazine.com/Reptile-Magazines/Reptiles-Magazine/July-2008/Breeding-Red-Eyed-Treefrogs/>

"Breeding Tree Frogs." Tree Frog Center. <http://www.treefrogcenter.com/breeding-tree-frogs.html>

"Captive Reptile & Amphibian Permit/License." Department of Natural Resources Maryland. <http://dnr.maryland.gov/wildlife/Pages/Licenses/captive.aspx>

"Chytridiomycosis." Wikipedia. <https://en.wikipedia.org/wiki/Chytridiomycosis>

"Common Diseases." CJSFrogs. <http://cjsfrogs.weebly.com/common-diseases.html>

"Deimatic Behaviour." Wikipedia.
<https://en.wikipedia.org/wiki/Deimatic_behaviour>

"Factors to Consider When Purchasing a Red Eyed Tree Frog." Red Eyed Tree Frog.
<http://www.redeyedtreefrog.org/factors-to-consider-when-purchasing-a-red-eyed-tree-frog/>

"Frog." Dictionary.com.
<http://www.dictionary.com/browse/frog>

"Frog." Wikipedia. <https://en.wikipedia.org/wiki/Frog>

"Frog Diet." Tree Frog Center.
<http://www.treefrogcenter.com/frog-diet.html>

"Frog Diseases: Fungal Infections." Frogworld.net.
<http://frogworld.net/health/fungal-infections.html>

"Frog Diseases: Metabolic Bone Disease (MBD)." Frogworld.net. <http://frogworld.net/health/mbd.html>

"Frog Diseases: Redleg." Frogworld.net.
<http://frogworld.net/health/redleg.html>

"Frog Feeding." Reptiles Info. <http://www.reptiles-info.co.uk/frog-feeding.html>

"Frog Keeper Licenses." NSW Office of Environment Heritage.
<http://www.environment.nsw.gov.au/wildlifelicences/frogkeeperslicence.htm>

"Glossary." Arkansas Frogs and Toads. <http://arkansasfrogsandtoads.org/frog-glossary/>

"Glossary." Froglife. <http://www.froglife.org/info-advice/glossary/>

"Glossary of Scientific Terms Used on AmphibiaWeb." AmphibiaWeb. <http://www.amphibiaweb.org/amphibian/glossary.html>

"How to Breed Red Eye Tree Frogs." Zbrinks. <http://www.joshsfrogs.com/catalog/blog/2016/04/breed-red-eye-tree-frogs/>

"How to breed Red-Eyed Treefrogs." Living with Lizards. <http://livingwithlizards.com/how-to-breed-red-eyed-treefrogs/>

"How to Build a Habitat for a Red-Eyed Tree Frog." Pets on Mom.Me. <http://animals.mom.me/build-habitat-redeyed-tree-frog-2368.html>

"How to Buy a Red Eyed Tree Frog." Red Eyed Tree Frog. <http://www.redeyedtreefrog.org/how-to-buy-a-red-eyed-tree-frog/>

"How to Recognize Illness in Red Eyed Tree Frog." Red Eyed Tree Frog. <http://www.redeyedtreefrog.org/how-to-recognize-illness-in-red-eyed-tree-frog/>

"How to Rescue These Adorable Tree Frogs." Brian Clark Howard.

<http://news.nationalgeographic.com/2016/04/160407-frog-rescue-chytrid-fungus-honduras-cusuco-jonathan-kolby/>

"Life Cycle of a Frog." All About Frogs. <http://allaboutfrogs.org/weird/general/cycle.html>

"Metabolic Bone Disease in Amphibians." PetMD. <http://www.petmd.com/reptile/conditions/musculoskelet al/c_rp_am_metabolic_bone>

"Nutrition." The Red-Eyed Tree Frog. <http://bioweb.uwlax.edu/bio203/s2007/bergin_lind/Nutriti on2.htm>

"Pet Care – Red Eyed Tree Frog." Froggyville. <http://www.froggyville.com/petcarered.htm>

"Pet Frog Cost." Cost Helper Pets & Pet Care. <http://pets.costhelper.com/frog.html>

"Red-eyed Tree Frog." Australian Museum. <https://australianmuseum.net.au/red-eyed-tree-frog>

"Red-eyed Tree Frog." Enchanted Learning.com. <http://www.enchantedlearning.com/subjects/amphibians/ redeyedtreefrog.shtml>

"Red-Eyed Tree Frog." National Geographic. <http://www.nationalgeographic.com/animals/amphibians /r/red-eyed-tree-frog/>

"Red-Eyed Tree Frog." Rainforest Alliance. <http://www.rainforest-alliance.org/species/tree-frog>

"Red-Eyed Tree Frog." Rainforest Animals.
<http://www.rainforestanimals.net/rainforestanimal/redey
edtreefrog.html>

"Red-Eyed Tree Frog." Redeyedtreefrogky.weebly.com.
<http://redeyedtreefrogky.weebly.com/life-cycle.html>

"Red Eyed Tree Frog." Regal Pet.
<http://regalpet.com/pets/668-red-eyed-tree-frog>

"Red-Eyed Tree Frog." Right Pet.
<https://rightpet.com/breed-species/amphibians/frogs/red-
eyed-tree-frog>

"Red-eyed Tree Frog." Switch Zoo.
<http://switchzoo.com/profiles/red-eyedtreefrog.htm>

"Red-Eyed Tree Frog." The Animal Spot.
<http://www.theanimalspot.com/redeyedtreefrog.htm>

"Red Eyed Tree Frog Activities in the Wild and in
Captivity." Red Eyed Tree Frog.
<http://www.redeyedtreefrog.org/activities-in-the-wild-
and-in-captivity/>

"Red-Eyed Tree Frog (Agalychnis calidryas)." Rainforest
Animals.
<http://www.rainforestanimals.net/rainforestanimal/redey
edtreefrog.html>

"Red Eyed Tree Frog: An Investigation." Olivia Selbie and Alyssa Shand-Perreault. <http://tolweb.org/treehouses/?treehouse_id=4841>

"Red Eyed Tree Frog Care Guide." ReptilesNCritters. <http://www.reptilesncritters.com/care-guide-red-eyed-tree-frogs.php>

"Red Eyed Tree Frog Fungal Disease." Red Eyed Tree Frog. <http://www.redeyedtreefrog.org/red-eyed-tree-frog-fungal-disease/>

"Red Eyed Tree Frog Housing." Reptiles Info. <http://www.reptiles-info.co.uk/frog-housing.html>

"Red-eyed Treefrog, Red-eyed Leaf-frog." The Red-Eyed Tree Frog Company. <http://www.redeyedtreefrog.com/Red-Eyed/red-eyed.html>

"Red eyed Tree Frog setup questions." Frog Forum. <http://www.frogforum.net/showthread.php?t=12770>

"Red Eyed Tree Frogs." LLL Reptile. <https://www.lllreptile.com/articles/116-red-eyed-tree-frogs/>

"Red-leg Syndrome." WikiVet. <https://en.wikivet.net/Red-leg_Syndrome>

"Sick Frogs and Salamanders." Philippe de Vosjoli. <http://www.reptilesmagazine.com/Frogs-Amphibians/Sick-Frogs-And-Amphibians/>

"The Life Cycle of a Red-eyed Tree Frog." Ricardo Gutierrez. <https://prezi.com/fpsqwnzjmj-k/the-life-cycle-of-a-red-eyed-tree-frog/>

"The Mixed Species Dilemma." Amphibian Care. <http://amphibiancare.com/2008/05/21/mixed-species-dilemma/>

"The Pros And Cons of Owning a Reptile or Amphibian." Pets Information. <http://pets.businessservices.esy.es/the-pros-and-cons-of-owning-a-reptile-or-amphibian/>

"The Pros & Cons of owning a Tree Frog." Hoverian. <http://hoverian.com/pets/the-pros-cons-of-owning-a-tree-frog/>

"The Red Eyed Tree Frog Poster: Art and Activism." Red Eyed Tree Frog. <http://www.redeyedtreefrog.org/the-red-eyed-tree-frog-poster-art-and-activism/>

"Top 4 Unique Characteristics of Red Eyed Tree Frogs." Red Eyed Tree Frog. <http://www.redeyedtreefrog.org/top-4-unique-characteristics-of-red-eyed-tree-frogs/>

"Tree Frog." Frog Life Cycle.com. <http://www.frog-life-cycle.com/tree-frog.html>

"Tree Frog Disease." Tree Frog Center. <http://www.treefrogcenter.com/tree-frog-disease.html>

"Tree Frogs – NA." Ectotherms Wiki. <http://ectotherms.wikia.com/wiki/Tree_Frogs_-_NA>

"Types of Red Eyed Tree Frog Health Issues." Red Eyed Tree Frog.org. <http://www.redeyedtreefrog.org/types-tree-frog-health-issues-diseases/>

"Vivarium & Habitat." Red Eyed Tree Frog. <http://www.redeyedtreefrog.org/frog-vivarium-tank-habitat/>

"What is a Frog's Transparent Eyelid Used For?" Pets on Mom.me. <http://animals.mom.me/frogs-transparent-eyelid-used-for-2504.html>

"Where to Buy a Red Eyed Tree Frog?" Red Eyed Tree Frog. <http://www.redeyedtreefrog.org/where-to-buy-a-red-eyed-tree-frog/>

"Winter is Coming: How do Frogs Avoid Freezing?" Frogs are Green. <http://frogsaregreen.org/tag/frogs-ectothermic-animal/>

"Your First Frog." All About Frogs. <http://allaboutfrogs.org/info/doctor/first.html>

Feeding Baby
Cynthia Cherry
978-1941070000

Axolotl
Lolly Brown
978-0989658430

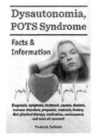

Dysautonomia, POTS
Syndrome
Frederick Earlstein
978-0989658485

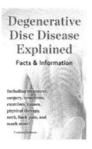

Degenerative Disc
Disease Explained
Frederick Earlstein
978-0989658485

Sinusitis, Hay Fever,
Allergic Rhinitis Explained
Frederick Earlstein
978-1941070024

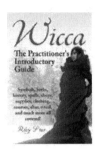

Wicca
Riley Star
978-1941070130

Zombie Apocalypse
Rex Cutty
978-1941070154

Capybara
Lolly Brown
978-1941070062

Eels As Pets
Lolly Brown
978-1941070167

Scabies and Lice Explained
Frederick Earlstein
978-1941070017

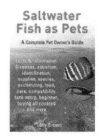

Saltwater Fish As Pets
Lolly Brown
978-0989658461

Torticollis Explained
Frederick Earlstein
978-1941070055

Kennel Cough
Lolly Brown
978-0989658409

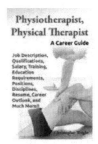

Physiotherapist, Physical
Therapist
Christopher Wright
978-0989658492

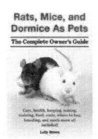

Rats, Mice, and Dormice
As Pets
Lolly Brown
978-1941070079

Wallaby and Wallaroo Care
Lolly Brown
978-1941070031

Bodybuilding Supplements
Explained
Jon Shelton
978-1941070239

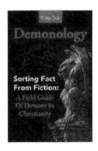

Demonology
Riley Star
978-19401070314

Pigeon Racing
Lolly Brown
978-1941070307

Dwarf Hamster
Lolly Brown
978-1941070390

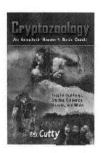

Cryptozoology
Rex Cutty
978-1941070406

Eye Strain
Frederick Earlstein
978-1941070369

Inez The Miniature Elephant
Asher Ray
978-1941070353

Vampire Apocalypse
Rex Cutty
978-1941070321

Made in the USA
San Bernardino, CA
08 August 2017